Which Egg Is Mine?

by Sheron Long

Illustrated by Lane Yerkes

HAMPTON-BROWN

A baby snake!
Oh, pardon me!
This egg isn't mine!

A baby turtle!
Oh, pardon me!
This egg isn't mine!

A baby lizard!
Oh, pardon me!
This egg isn't mine!

A baby duck!
Oh, pardon me!
This egg isn't mine!

A baby spider!
Oh, pardon me!
This egg isn't mine!

A baby chick!
At last!
This egg is mine.

And so are all of these!